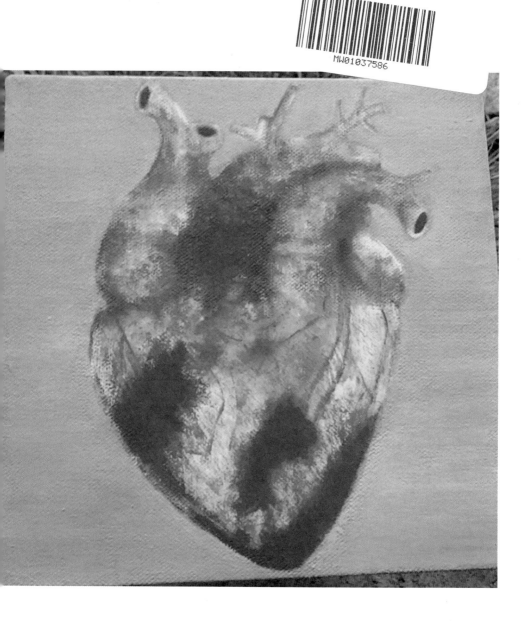

# *A Hue Of Blue*
# *BY Anastasia*

# A Hue Of Blue
## Poems, painting, and Layout
### By Anastasia Chacon

*Dedicated to all my loved ones whom helped me through these 29 years of life, and to all who keep the breath flowing through my lungs. I love you.*
*And to the reader who has felt anguish and pain in the heart, I hope these poems are a comfort to you. Thank you.*
*Love, Anastasia*

# Table of contents:

*My whole life rejected and told what to do, everywhere I go, so bare with me, my metaphors are true*
*Denied my color, hated it, didn't want to play that role*
*Scared of it, the truth that is*
*Now full on acceptance, there is nothing left to do, my brain has it*
*It is implanted*
*This feeling seems so normal hence, I come off like the Mad Hatter*
*Attracting blue situations, never good enough, I cry*
*All these blues and I've played them all*
*I am a broken ruined crayon and your least favorite color*
*This numbness, this shield, I can't remember when it was built*
*Perhaps, the first time my heart ached*
*It could be from that one time I tried to make it*
*Scrounging the earth for love, I cry to above, I am blue! I am hurt!*
*I am forever left needing and feigning for love*
*This is just part of life you say… But, no, it isn't, It is insanity, a  will for torture*
*And, I can't stop tasting it, I swallow more and more,*
*Along with you and the many many shades of blue*


**Blue (1**

*When the heart is broken*
*A human can turn into a variety different things*
*A monster is just one*

**Monster Heart (2**

*My heart beats in the rhythm of happiness and I am tuned to the note of love*
*I am in love with myself and another*
*I am older and I am wiser*
*I know who you are, because I know who I am*
*I have come to recognize my demons, so that I can see all of yours*
*I can say I trust myself and mean it*
*I see behind it all*
*The falling together*
*How we are all one*
*I understand you*
*But, if I can not teach you, I will leave you to learn*
*... A moment of light, a sniff of clarity*
*Lord, I've become conscious*

**The Wise Woman (3**

*Your name,*
*Your presence,*
*The thought of you,*
*And you entirely*
*Makes my heart beat a certain way*
*Saying I love you diminishes the feeling*
*Then I realized,*
*That you are my whole heart*
*Beat and all*

*~ You are my whole entire heart, beat and all*

**Marissa (4**

*Book open*
*Pen in hand*
*Yet, nothing to put down*
*Heart pumping*
*But, not for you anymore*
*So, what do I write about now*
*When I have no muse*
*What do I write about*
*When my heart is bruised and blue*
*And nothing good comes out*
*Open book*
*Pen in hand*
*I'm afraid that's all I have*

**Muse (5**

*As much as I've tried*
*As much as I've given it thought*
*As many times as I've had the opportunity*
*I still can't ever change my penguin heart to form into any other animal*
*To lower myself from something rare to something so common as to a dog*
*No matter what, it will always and only ever be you*
*My penguin*

**Penguin Heart (6**

*The heart wants a beat which understands*
*A sense of comfort, in means of a real man*

**A Real Man (7**

*When you walked away*
*I thought I lost everything*
*My heart ached*
*And the will to live was crushed by all my pain*
*I called out your name*
*But, you just continued walking*
*As if I was nobody*
*As if I was nothing*

**Memories (8**

*As gravity wins the battle against my tears*
*I feel this is what heartache must be*
*A cold broken glass full of air in my chest*
*A still quiet weep*
*Who knew*
*Who knew that I loved him*

**Who Knew (9**

*I've heard people speak of the cold before*
*Of this darkness, I've listened*
*But, to feel it myself when you are oh so near*
*To feel this, what is almost like moisture on my skin*
*This chill*
*I am cold now*
*My heart is black*
*And I don't like it*

**A Black Kind Of Pain (10**

*You'll never know how many tears I've cried*
*You'll never know how many times I wiped my own eyes*
*You'll never know just how much I would hide*
*You'll never understand how you washed me dry*
*You won't ever know the storm that resided inside*
*How I wept in that bed, how I drenched my whole head*
*How I begged to God on my knees, to please, make you understand me*
*The rain in my soul, right from the start, when I saw you couldn't love me,*
*When I saw it was too late, for heaven's sake, how I couldn't give up,*
*Oh, how you broke my heart*
*The times I died, deep down inside*
*The ugly I felt throughout those cold nights*
*Fighting with myself, justifying why*
*Abandoned in the dark*
*I didn't get how someone I loved so much can mess me up this bad in the head*
*Why God, why did I ever let him in*
*Why have I sinned against my own self*
*The pain was never worth it, not ever, not an ounce*

**You will never know (11**

*The heart wants what it wants*
*Yet, feels the tumbles and stumbles of pain while wanting it*
*It cannot change itself*
*Nor, can the brain help*
*While the body pays the consequences of tosses and turns,*
*My heart still wants what it wants*
*But, this affliction my whole being can do nothing about*

**Stubborn Kind Heart (12**

When my heart hurts and my chest aches
And I know I shouldn't be awake
While the world sleeps, at such an hour, I'm wide awake, yet so tired
As my mind races and demons taunting
Memories of you leave me wanting
I fall to my knees to pray, to cry, to ask God why
I toss and turn until morning, still not knowing, still broken and open
All the while you're somewhere else distracted, living, and smiling
While I do all of the crying, all of the weeping, and all of the sighing

**An unfair love (13**

*And there goes my heart doing that butterfly thing again*
*When it skips a beat and sort of feels like a balloon*
*All at the mention of you*

**Mi Mariposa (14**

*I am human*
*So cliche, so cliche*
*I am rotten, yet beautiful at once*
*Evil broods in my mind, but I speak wisdom*
*My heart is full of blackness from what I know*
*But, there has never been this much to love*
*I believe in children, mermaids, and God*
*I am a creature capable of hating one's self*
*The same creature who can only care about pleasing itself*
*I am someone's lover, sister, friend, daughter, and aunt*
*And I love what I equal with you all*
*I am deeply sorry for being selfish, for getting lost, and for any moment I wasn't there*
*I am so complicated*
*I have done everything I said I would not do*
*I have no regrets*
*But, Lord, I am sorry*
*I am little*
*A little nothing in this space of time*
*A nothing with expression*
*Hence, this poem*
*I can be nothing and mean everything*
*I am human*

**I am Human (15**

*My heart*

*My heart has begun to roll*

*It is changing with the wind*

*With time*

*My mind has no control over just and only this*

*For, my heart has been bruised*

*Its been used and not listened to*

*Its been dumb and its been numb*

*But, now it seems as though it is done*

*My heart is my heart*

*At times my only friend*

*For it to say enough, must mean this is the end*

*So, here is my heart trying words once again*

*With some hurt and a little pain*

*I'm sorry, I hope you can understand*

*Signed, sincerely, My Heart*

**My Heart (16**

*I know you are fine, I know you are strong*

*I have faith that you will find your happiness and where you belong*

*I must let go*

*For, life needs to unfold*

*Wherever I be, if you can not reach me please, don't take it personally*

*I know you are smart, I know you are strong*

*Seek after your heart*

*Never do what feels wrong*

*I hate goodbyes, but there is justice in this one*

*Goodbye my old friend*

*It's okay that we never meet again*

*I know you are fine, this isn't wrong*

*We shared something that should be learned from*

*It's time to move on, not looking back*

*And, perhaps, eventually even forget*

*This is the road that is next*

*I hope you can be your best, caring friend*

*I know you will make it*

*I never needed to hold your hand*

*I know you will find love and yourself once again*

**He's Fine (17**

*You are the only warmth in my heart in this death of a world*
*You are the light that keeps me going while I walk through the dark*
*You are my joy even when I've lost it all*
*Your voice is my comfort, like a receiving blanket is to an infant*
*Your touch is almost what a breath is*
*In this most stormy life, at the very least I can take pride in saying that you are mine*
*In this most stormy life, I must remember that God made you mine*

**Family (18**

As my heart beats against gravity

As it pounds with each afflicted breath I breathe, I aim towards thee

I hope my Father in heaven will avenge me

I've never felt such anguish

I've never expected such life

I'm not the type to woe, nor ask why

But, to make you understand, you'd be near dying

To make you understand, you'd go on crying

If you understood, you would never look at me the same

You would stop with all of your real life games

You would have no one but yourself to blame

I rather stop mid life, then to go on with such strife

Then to go on with such a mind

I pray that God can make you see

I pray that He will avenge me

**HIs Real Life Games (19**

*Lord knows*

*I've written and written*

*I've even wrote a song out of my poetry*

*Took it and sang my heart out*

*As if exhaling every word meant that you were leaving me*

*All the while, it did feel good*

*But, when it is all said and done*

*And I lie here at night*

*I find that you,*

*That you still linger*

**Lingering (20**

*The flesh is of a great desire, it is ever wanting more*

*Yet, this seeming full, ample device still can't satisfy my soul*

*So, how can one not see the truth?*

*For, it is plain and simple, without deceit*

*In my heart I know I don't belong here,*

*Not one minute, not no more*

*This flesh I fight, both day and night,*

*This demon will always be deficient*

*I must cut it off*

*As my essence knows, again, this is not my home*

*My home is in heaven*

*Only there will I be truly happy and complete*

*Till then I must guard my salvation*

*Sin, I shall not*

*For, my home is in heaven*


**Anastasia's Truth (21**

*I'll always remember you*
*And you will always have a place in my heart*
*Because, it is in your home*
*Where I truly began to heal and find myself*

**Peri And Pastor (22**

Made in United States
Orlando, FL
07 April 2024

45562212R00015